PENGUIN BOOKS

DARLING, I LOVE YOU

DANIEL LADINSKY is one of the most successful living writers in the world working with poetry. His work has reached millions of people. Daniel lived in India for six years, where he volunteered in a rural clinic, free to the poor, and was a student of the essence and unity of all faiths. Ladinsky's other Penguin books include *The Gift, Love Poems from God, The Subject Tonight Is Love, I Heard God Laughing, A Year with Hafiz,* and his Rumi collection, *The Purity of Desire.* Once, when Daniel was asked a reason for his accomplishments and whether he had any advice for other artists, he quoted a line from an old Broadway musical that went, "You've gotta have heart, miles and miles and miles of heart!"

PATRICK McDONNELL is the creator of the comic strip *MUTTS*, which debuted in 1994 and appears in over seven hundred newspapers in twenty-two countries. *MUTTS* has been anthologized in twenty-five books in the United States and in numerous collections throughout the world. He has created a dozen children's books, including the Caldecott Honor–winning *Me . . . Jane,* a biography of Jane Goodall, and the *New York Times* bestselling *The Gift of Nothing.* McDonnell collaborated with Eckhart Tolle on *Guardians of Being: Spiritual Teachings from Our Dogs and Cats.* He is a member of the board of directors of the Humane Society of the United States, the Fund for Animals, and the Charles M. Schulz Museum.

Also by Daniel Ladinsky

The Gift:
Poems by Hafiz, the Great Sufi Master

Love Poems from God:
Twelve Sacred Voices from the East and West

The Subject Tonight Is Love:
60 Wild and Sweet Poems of Hafiz

I Heard God Laughing:
Poems of Hope and Joy

A Year with Hafiz:
Daily Contemplations

The Purity of Desire:
100 Poems of Rumi
(with Nancy Owen Barton)

Darling, I Love You

*Poems from the Hearts of
Our Glorious Mutts
and All Our Animal Friends*

DANIEL LADINSKY

Illustrated by
PATRICK McDONNELL

PENGUIN BOOKS

PENGUIN BOOKS
An imprint of Penguin Random House LLC
penguinrandomhouse.com

"The Sacraments," "First He Looked Confused," and "Does Every Creature Have
a Soul?" appeared in *Love Poems from God: Twelve Sacred Voices from the East
and West* (Penguin Books). Copyright © 2002 by Daniel Ladinsky.

"The Anointment," "One Regret," and "Adios" appeared in *A Year with Hafiz:
Daily Contemplations* (Penguin Books). Copyright © 2011 by Daniel Ladinsky.

"Just Sit There" appeared in *The Subject Tonight Is Love: 60 Wild and Sweet Poems
of Hafiz* (Penguin Books). Copyright © 2003 by Daniel Ladinsky.

LIBRARY OF CONGRESS CATALOGING-IN-PUBLICATION DATA
Names: Ladinsky, Daniel James, author. | McDonnell, Patrick, 1956– illustrator.
Title: Darling, I love you : poems from the hearts of our glorious mutts and
all our animal friends / Daniel Ladinsky ; illustrated by Patrick McDonnell.
Description: New York : Penguin Books, [2017]
Identifiers: LCCN 2016032732 (print) | LCCN 2016036648 (ebook) | ISBN
9780143128267 (paperback) | ISBN 9780698407336 (ebook)
Subjects: LCSH: Human-animal relationships—Poetry. | Pets—Poetry | BISAC:
POETRY / American / General. | PETS / Essays. | HUMOR / Form / Comic
Strips & Cartoons.
Classification: LCC PS3612.A365 A6 2017 (print) | LCC PS3612.A365 (ebook) |
DDC 811/.6—dc23

Printed in the United States of America

Set in Bembo
Design by Jeff Schulz

A CONVERSATION BETWEEN LOVERS

I have been working with the fourteenth-century Persian poet Hafiz for twenty-five years, along with other great poet-saints East and West. Some of my work with them appears in my best-selling Penguin anthology, *Love Poems from God*. I try to bring to life their wonderful spirit and reveal something of their remarkable giving heart and vital compassion, and their gift of genius to the world, as Ralph Waldo Emerson and Goethe attempted with Hafiz. Hafiz was a master of wit, profundity, and love, and a few lines of his, as rendered by me, seem appropriate here:

> Art is a conversation between lovers,
> art can open the door to many suns.

> Art can stir the divine silence in the
> soul to sing in an ecstatic applause.

> The beauty of art is it helps us to know
> our own wonder, and that in all that is.

May something in this sweet and beautiful book aid your wings in tasting the sky and to blessedly smile. And I bet Rumi and Hafiz—and Saint Francis, whose work I have also interpreted—would have bowed to dear Patrick, *and maybe do*, who protects so many of God's creatures with his great talents, and life.

— Daniel Ladinsky
Taos, New Mexico, 2016

WORDS AND PICTURES

Comic strips and haiku are, in some ways, kindred spirits. Whether it's three panels or seventeen syllables, they can say a lot with a little. The cartoonist and the poet both chip away at their work in order to reveal its essence. As you continue to refine and "let go," you ultimately discover that the only thing left standing is love.

Daniel's poems magically capture these precious moments of clarity and bliss. His words bring us presence and an inner smile with the same ease and playfulness as our beloved companion animals.

It was a joy and honor to have the *MUTTS* gang be a part of his world.

Let these poems curl up on your lap and soothe your heart.

Yep.

— Patrick McDonnell

love is respecting
the beings who can't speak
and treating them

as if
they
could

Begin the Beguine

have you
ever heard of
Cole Porter?

i am not sure?

he wrote
that very famous song
Begin the Beguine

there is a line
in that song that
maybe *all* —

the mountains
and the sky and the rivers
and the oceans

and all the forests
and all the deserts
and all the fields

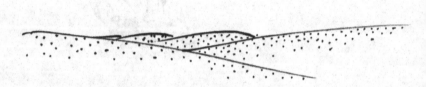

and all the planets
and all the
flowers

and all the animals,
yes, all the *animals*
and all the fish —

sing to us
all day long, but we just
can't hear them

well, what line is that?

Darling, I love you!

i think we should
always sing that to
each other,

and i
will start
right now:

O, darling, i loooooooooooove you!

i love my wanting

i love
my wanting to be
with you

and i love
my being there

thoughts from a cat

why can
i sit so still
for so long

and
look
content?

because
i know a few
things

one of the top ten things in a dog's life: *fetch*

if it wasn't
for fetch i would
never be

the wonderful
being
i am

without question

great things sometimes
are done in this world
without question

or
hesitation,
like

me jumping
into your
lap

talk of the town

i had a bird for
a girlfriend once; we became
the talk of the town

a child at a circus

like a child
at a circus,
i am in awe

of the postman
driving by

 and people
walking past

and that squirrel
on a
limb

and the sound
of a pot in
the kitchen

and the water
sprinkler

and my own
breathing

in the moment

you should try
being in the moment,

then you'd
want to catch
things

in *your*
mouth
too!

a friend

sometimes all you need
is a friend who won't
question you

revelations or insights

how did
you sleep
last night?

*better
than
usual . . .*

any
revelations or
great insights?

*revelations
or
insights!*

that's getting
too heavy for my
simple routine —
at 7:42 AM

well,
did you have
any?

i love
sleeping

a touch

a touch that
quiets, where else
to go

even in my water bowl

even in
my water bowl the
moon can fit

belly rub

when you ask
for a belly rub
like that

i am glad
to realize

you are the *king*
and i just a lucky
servant

acting afraid

you were acting
afraid in a dream so
i kissed you awake

noble thoughts

my first thoughts
in the morning are:
i am ready for love . . .

i am one of its
warriors,

i am
one of its
heroes,

i will die
for love, and *do*
as we do —

in some ways
every day.

after such true
and noble thoughts

then it is usually
time for a #1 and
#2 . . .

that helps
to balance
my otherwise

near
continuous
exalted condition

like them

not wanting to
make humans
feel bad . . .

i might pretend
barking up the wrong
tree *sometimes*

like
them

what more

an ear twitched,
i watched my paw move,
what more could i want

magic

sometimes
i wonder if i
am magic . . .

seeing how those
who touch me start
to smile

a good guess

being a stray,
it is a little iffy as
to my birthday . . .

but the vet
made a good guess
we all now go with

moon whispers

the moon sometimes
whispers the sweetest things
in my ear

i am so glad

start seeing everything as God,
but keep it a secret.

become like a man who is awestruck
and nourished

listening to a golden nightingale
sing in a beautiful foreign language
while God invisibly nests
upon its tongue.

who can you tell in this world
that when a dog runs up to you
wagging its ecstatic tail,
you lean down and whisper in its ear,

"Beloved,
i am so glad You are happy to see me.

Beloved,
i am so glad,
so very glad You have come."

heaven is

heaven is
a little stuffed dog
in your mouth

she phoned saying

she phoned saying,

"i will
be over in a
minute,"

but the sweet snail
was just figuratively
speaking

of
course

sit

i could *sit too*
if you asked sweetly
and offered

a
glazed
donut

dragonfly wings

hovering over the lake
those dragonfly wings
i found . . . are working

can't you see

can't you see that
look in my eye that
belly rub *causes* . . .

so
why ever
stop?

help out around the house

i would like
to help out around
the house more

if they
would let
me.

in a way
it does not
seem fair

all the
time off
i get

going so fast

i wonder
where everyone
is going so fast . . .

and then
once
there . . .

probably still
feel anxious about
something

scratching

scratching my back
against the moon,
my yoga

the park

the dog park,
the dog park,
the glorious dog park . . .

need
anyone ever, ever & *ever*
say more

gee whiz

i saw the moon wink
last night! gee whiz, i will
never be the same

golden

that bone as
golden as anything
right now

gratias

food in my bowl
caring sounds
gentle hands

no longer alone
on the street weeping
at times

if you see me
kneeling in
prayer,

repeating
for
days

gratias
gratias, gratias
gratias

never
wonder
why

the path to wholeness

along the path to
wholeness one makes all
creatures near *feel safe*

the sky

the sky is
a suspended
blue ocean

and the stars
are the fish that
swim

car ride?

"do you want
to go for a car ride?"
mom said . . .

and i
thought to myself . . .
hasn't she

seen those ecstatic
drool stains on the door
under the window . . .

i
call my
own . . .

and
ever willing
to add to

all is rigged

looks like
you are cruising
today.

yep, I figured out
Rumi wasn't jiving
when he said,
"All is rigged in our favor!"

circled

this place where
you are *right now* —
God

circled on a
map for
you

in the loop

the moon
lets me in the loop
on lots of stuff

awesome surprise

awesome surprise
when the sky lifted me
into its arms

and told me
it had been waiting
so long

the sacraments

i once spoke to my friend,
an old squirrel,
about the sacraments —

he got so excited
and ran
into a hollow in his tree

and came back
holding some acorns,

an owl feather,

and a ribbon he had found.

and i just smiled and said,
"yes, dear, you understand:

everything imparts
His grace."

tears

i have been
moved to tears
thinking

about
a chew
toy

the friend

why go into the city
or the field without first
kissing the Friend

who always
stands at your
door

love lifts

love

lifts the corners

of the mouth

fun

have fun, my dear,
my dear, have

fun

yep

no fake
kisses from
us dogs

our time
is too precious

yep

feral

i wonder if the
moon is a feral cat
like me

two soft eyes & trust

what could be more humbling
than the devotion of your
two soft eyes

melting
into
me

and something
as sacred as you
trusting my care

have a heart

all creatures say,

i have a heart, i can know

happiness like you

greet yourself

greet yourself
in your thousand
other forms

fully at play

love
is all beings
being

fully at play
with no dogcatchers
around

bumped heads

once the moon
and i bumped heads
looking into a lake

your heart and my heart

your heart and my heart
are very, very old
friends

first he looked confused

i could not lie anymore
so i started to call my dog
"God."

first he looked
confused,

then he started smiling,
then he even
danced.

i kept at it:
now he doesn't even
bite.

i am wondering if this
might work on
people?

tattooed

a rainbow
tattooed itself
to a trout

angel

i know what i am
to some, a wingless
angel

the anointment

dear ones,
let's anoint this earth with

dance!

the ordinary

the ordinary
never ceases
to be extraordinary

wall flowers

once it occurred
to me the stars were
something like

wall
flowers

and that next
time a tune moved
my feet at night

i should ask
a couple to
dance

wagging ecstatic

i broke an
antique lamp last night
wagging ecstatic

a sweet bark

just thought
i'd toss a sweet
bark in

loving everything

loving everything as she was

the goldfish's bowl turned

into the ocean

confused

if i ever look confused
it is because love is playing

hide & seek

new things

the heart that
discovers new things
can glow

quiet here

quiet here
with the moon holding
me so close

the art of digging holes

life can be like
digging holes in your
backyard

sometimes
it doesn't make
much sense

but we
keep doing
it

say ahhhhh

do you think
the Buddha ever
pinched you?

how could one
ever know such
a thing?

'cause then you
start being able to
kick back more . . .

and
say
ahhhhhh

while together

while together
let us say something
that warms us

simple things

it's the simple things
that never get old

my dear

my dear,
how can i be more
loving to you;

how can i be more
kind?

moon tows

the moon tows
the oceans and soooo
many hearts

a sweet story

the crickets
are telling a sweet
story

give his ears a rub

wherever you are . . .
give God's furry ears
a rub

guess most everything has its limits

the moon
thanked me for
a song i sang

sooooo
i belted out
another one

then i had
in mind
a third

but she must
have read my
thoughts . . .

and said,
time to cool
it.

guess most
everything has
its limits

so i did

when there was
no other hand to help
you move on

i offered
you
four,

well,
furry paws they
were . . .

but full of such
strength like my heart's
precious *shelter*

'cause love says,
*i will, i will take care
of you,*

so
i
did . . .

so i did
my
love

a cozy place

looks like a
cozy place to sleep
at night . . .

indeed, and sometimes
my sweetheart covers me
with a golden leaf

tucked in

last night
the snow tucked in
some forest creatures

one regret

one regret that
i am determined not
to have

is that i did
not kiss you
enough

just sit there

just sit there right now.
don't do a thing.
just rest.

for your separation from God
is the hardest work in this world.

let me bring you trays of food
and something
that you like to drink.

you can use my soft words
as a cushion
for your
head.

outer space

i am starting to
believe all *outer space*
is really inside

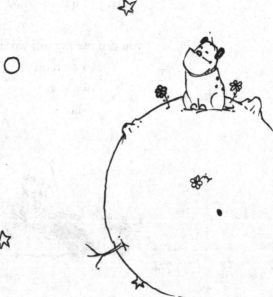

never be less furry

that you — God —
would never be
any less furry,
and always accessible
and loving as
my cat;

and like her,
sleep with your head
on my shoulder.

and, of course,
don't forget the

purrrrrrrrr!

littermates

littermates
all of us,
really

surely they do

a tool
in your hand i am, dear God,
the sweetest instrument
you have shaped my being into.

what makes me now complete —
feeling the soul of every creature
against my heart.

does every creature have a soul?

surely they do;
for anything God has touched
will have life
forever,

and all creatures He
has held.

adios

not wanting
to seem impolite
when the deer

ran off, she raised
her beautiful white tail
and waved . . .

good-bye

O, darling, i loooooooooooove you!

ACKNOWLEDGMENTS

I feel a real synergy happened here with Patrick McDonnell and me. I think we have created quite a significant little party & oasis in this book, one that I hope many will visit for years & years. My tremendous thanks to Patrick—and his grand art, and to his wife, Karen, in allowing me to be a part of this wonderful project and dream Patrick and I have both shared for some time now.

Also, I want to so thank Melissa LaScaleia—and her nimble Harvard brain—for some of her verse that landed in this book verbatim, and several others of hers that she and I collaborated on. She was working with me as an assistant, and in a blind test we slipped some of her work with haiku & renga into the over 1000 we submitted to Patrick for this volume. And Melissa and I both felt so happy when Patrick chose several of hers to go to press. So keep writing, Melissa . . . bet Matsuo Bashō would want ya to!

And Nancy Barton, my agent at times, consultant, and talented old friend, got one or two of hers in here via some kind of cat or dog door . . . off the kitchen. Thanks, Nancy, for your contribution and for sticking by my side for so many years.

And Henry Dunow and Meg Leder deserve a giant bravo! O yeah!

Love to you, and a big hug, and thanks,

— Daniel

My deepest gratitude and appreciation to —

Daniel, for his creativity, enthusiasm, generosity, and trust.
I feel our hearts are "very, very old friends."

Meg Leder and Patrick Nolan at Penguin.

Designer Jeff Schulz,
agents Henry Dunow and Nancy Barton,
and, of course, my Karen.

I'd like to dedicate these illustrated prayers to Mr. Kitty, Mrs. Kitty,
Spooky, Earl, MeeMow, Not Ootie, Amelie, and all animals everywhere.

Gratias.

— Patrick